Modern Curriculum Press
BEGINNING
TO
READ
Series

MODERN CURRICULUM PRESS

You Are Here, Dainty Dinosaur

by

Babs Bell Hajdusiewicz

illustrated by Diana Noro

ISBN: 0-8136-5714-8
Printed in the United States of America

5 6 7 8 9 10   06 05 04 03 02

Modern
Curriculum
Press

Pearson Learning Group

1-800-321-3106
www.pearsonlearning.com

What is this?
What is this I see?
I will get it.

I like it.
It is so pretty.
It will go home with me.

Look!
Look here!
See what I have!
See the spots.

Oh, that is pretty.
It is dainty.
What will you do with that dainty thing?

Dainty?
What is "dainty"?
Is that pretty?

9

Yes and no.
See.
This is dainty.
And it is pretty.

That is pretty.
But it is not dainty.
That is pretty, too.
But not dainty.
Your thing looks pretty
and dainty.

You are my dainty thing.
I will put you there.
I like you, dainty thing.
You have spots like I have.

Oh.

What is this?

That was not there.

But it is there now.

Did I do that to you?

Here.
I will put you down, my dainty thing.

I have to go now.
I have to get something.
I will be back.

Here I come, dainty thing.
Here I come to see you.

Oh, my!
What is this?
My dainty thing!
What did you do?

I see you.
I see you back there.
Did you come out of my dainty thing?

Oh!
There you are.
Look at you.

Come here.
Come here.
We can be friends.

See.
My house will be your house.
Will you play with me?

Look at you!
You have blue spots
on your back.
I have spots too.

My, my!
You are a dinosaur!
A dinosaur is not dainty.
But you were in my dainty thing.
So you will be my
Dainty Dinosaur!
You will like it here
with me.

Come, Dainty Dinosaur.
I want you to see your house.
I eat in here.
Do you want to eat?

This is good to eat.
I like it.
You will like it, too.

Oh, Dainty Dinosaur!
Where did it go?
You *do* like it!

I play in here.
See.
I can play that.

What?
You can play, too?
That is pretty.
I like it, my Dainty Dinosaur.

Look.
This is me.
See my spots.
And this is you.
Do you see you
and me?

My Dainty Dinosaur.
You are you.
And I am me.
You are here with me.
I love you, Dainty
Dinosaur.
I love you so!

Babs Bell Hajdusiewicz, author and poet, is the originator of Pee Wee Poetry™. She is a former teacher and school administrator and lives in Rocky River, Ohio.

You Are Here, Dainty Dinosaur uses the 66 words listed below.

a		that
am	I	the
and	in	there
are	is	thing (s)
at	it	this
		to
back	like	too
be	look (s)	
blue	love	
but		up
	me	
can	my	want
come		was
	no	were
dainty	not	what
did	now	where
dinosaur		will
do	of	with
down	oh	
	on	
eat	out	yes
		you
		your
friend (s)	play	
	pretty	
get	put	
go		
good	see	
	so	
have	something	
here	spot (s)	
home		
house		